FUN FACTS!

THE FIRST DEPICTION OF A SNOWMAN WAS IN 1380 AD. (THE "BOOK OF HOURS")
POSITIVELY MEDIEVAL!

PG. 1

FiND YOUR WAY TO THE SNOWMAN!

HERE I AM!

THE FIRST PHOTO OF A SNOWMAN WAS IN 1853!

150 YEARS BEFORE SELFIES! SADLY, NO FILTERS EITHER

FUN FACTS!

THE WORLD'S BIGGEST SNOWMAN IS ALMOST
AS TALL AS THE STATUE OF LIBERTY!
GIVE ME YOUR TIRED, YOUR POOR,
YOUR CHILLED TO THE BONE!

FUN FACTS: THE WORLD'S SMALLEST SNOWMAN WAS MADE USING NANO-TECHNOLOGY! ♪ TINY BUBBLES 🎵

PG 5

FUN FACTS!

A WOMAN IN MINNESOTA HAS THE WORLD'S LARGEST COLLECTION OF SNOWMEN - 5,127 PIECES! EVERYONE NEEDS A HOBBY!

FUN FACTS:

THE MOST SNOWMEN BUILT IN AN HOUR
- 2,036. BY HAND!

COOL! A SNOWMAN GARDEN!

FUN FACTS:

"FROSTY THE SNOWMAN" (RANKIN & BASS)
FIRST AIRED ON T.V. IN 1969
"FROSTY THE OLD MAN" YOU MEAN

PG 8

FUN FACTS:

ON THE FIRST DAY OF SPRING, AT "HIGH NOON" LAKE SUPERIOR UNIVERSITY BURNS A PAPER SNOWMAN   HOT! HOT! HOT!

PG 9

FUN FACTS:

SNOWMEN HAVE EVEN BEEN BUILT TO GUARD
A FORT FROM ATTACK (IT DIDN'T WORK!)
HALT! WHO GOES THERE?

PG 10

FUN FACTS!

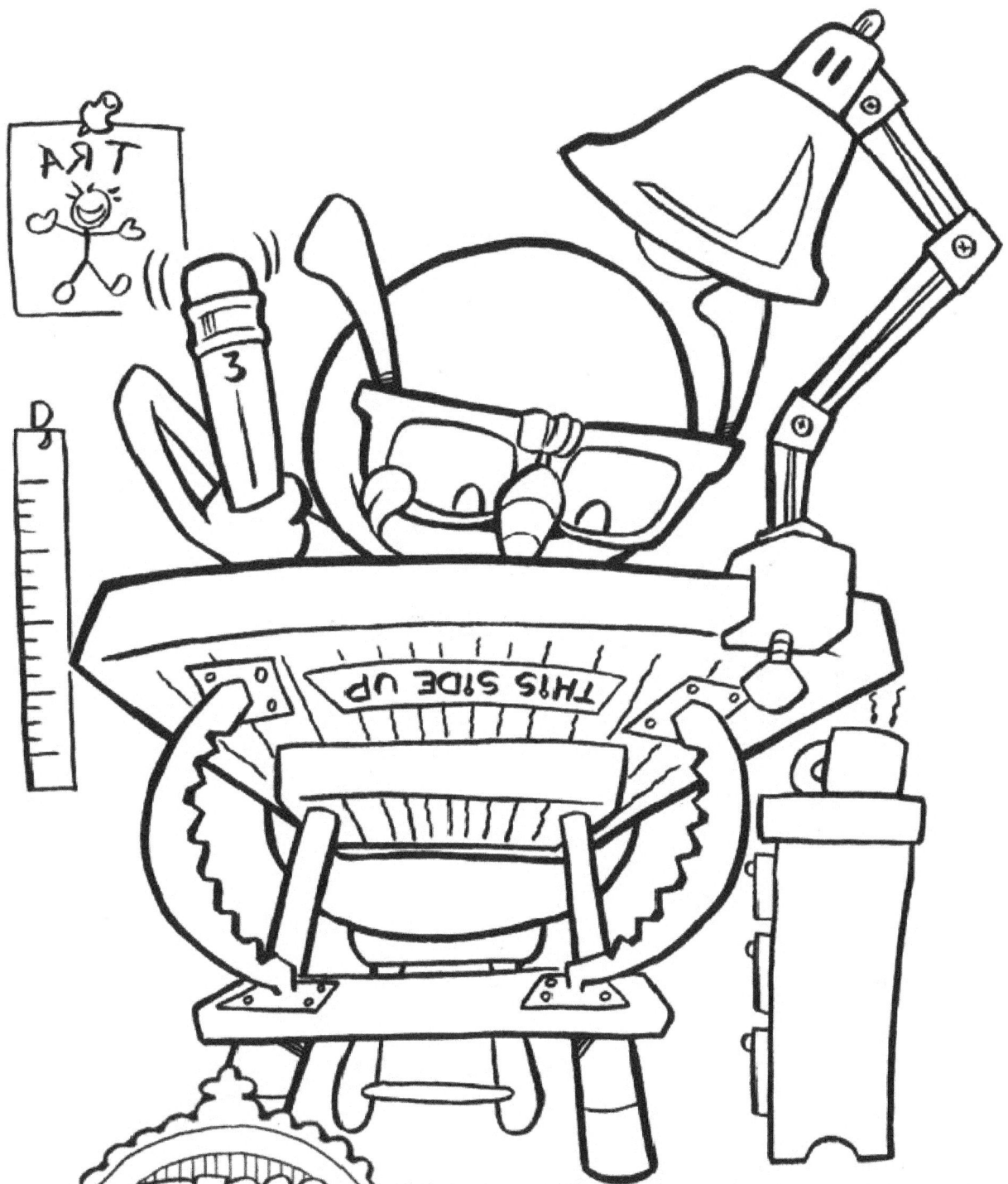

EVEN MICHELANGELO WAS COMMISSIONED
TO BUILD A SNOWMAN! (1494)

SO KEEP DRAWING!!

PG 11

FUN FACTS!

THERE ARE MORE THAN 90 THOUSAND VIDEO'S
ON HOW TO BUILD A SNOWMAN!

HOPE YOU LIKE TO BINGE WATCH

FUN FACTS:

THE TALLEST EVER SNOWMAN WAS 125FT!
AND USED TREES FOR ARMS!
GIMME A HUG

PG 13

PG 14

FUN FACTS!

EVERY YEAR, IN ZURICH, "BÖÖGG" THE SNOWMAN IS PARADED THROUGH THE STREETS - WHILE BREAD AND SAUSAGE IS THROWN TO THE CROWD
WHAT? NO KETCHUP?

FUN FACTS!

THE TALLEST SNOW-WOMAN, IN BETHEL MAINE, WAS 122FT!

HER YOGA PANTS WERE HUMUNGEOUS!

PG 15

FUN FACTS:

THE STORY OF "FROSTY THE SNOWMAN" (BOOK) CAME OUT IN 1950

STILL DANCING AROUND - AT YOUR AGE?

PG 16

FUN FACTS:

75% OF ALL FRESH WATER COMES FROM
SNOW AND ICE!
DRINK UP!

PG 17

FUN FACTS:

IN SWITZERLAND THEY CELEBRATE THE START OF SPRING BY BLOWING UP SNOWMEN!

"FIRE IN THE HOLE!"

PG 18

FUN FACTS!

IN THE SWISS FESTIVAL - THE TIME IT TAKES FOR THE SNOWMAN TO EXPLODE IS SAID TO PREDICT THE ARRIVAL OF SPRING   6 MORE WEEKS OF TNT!

FUN FACTS:

IN 1511, IN BRUSSELS BELGIUM -
110 SNOWMEN MELTED - CAUSING A FLOOD!
COWABUNGA, DUDE

PG 20

FUN FACTS:

SNOW IS ACTUALLY TRANSPARENT!

CAN YOU SAY SPF 9000?

PG 21

FUN FACTS!

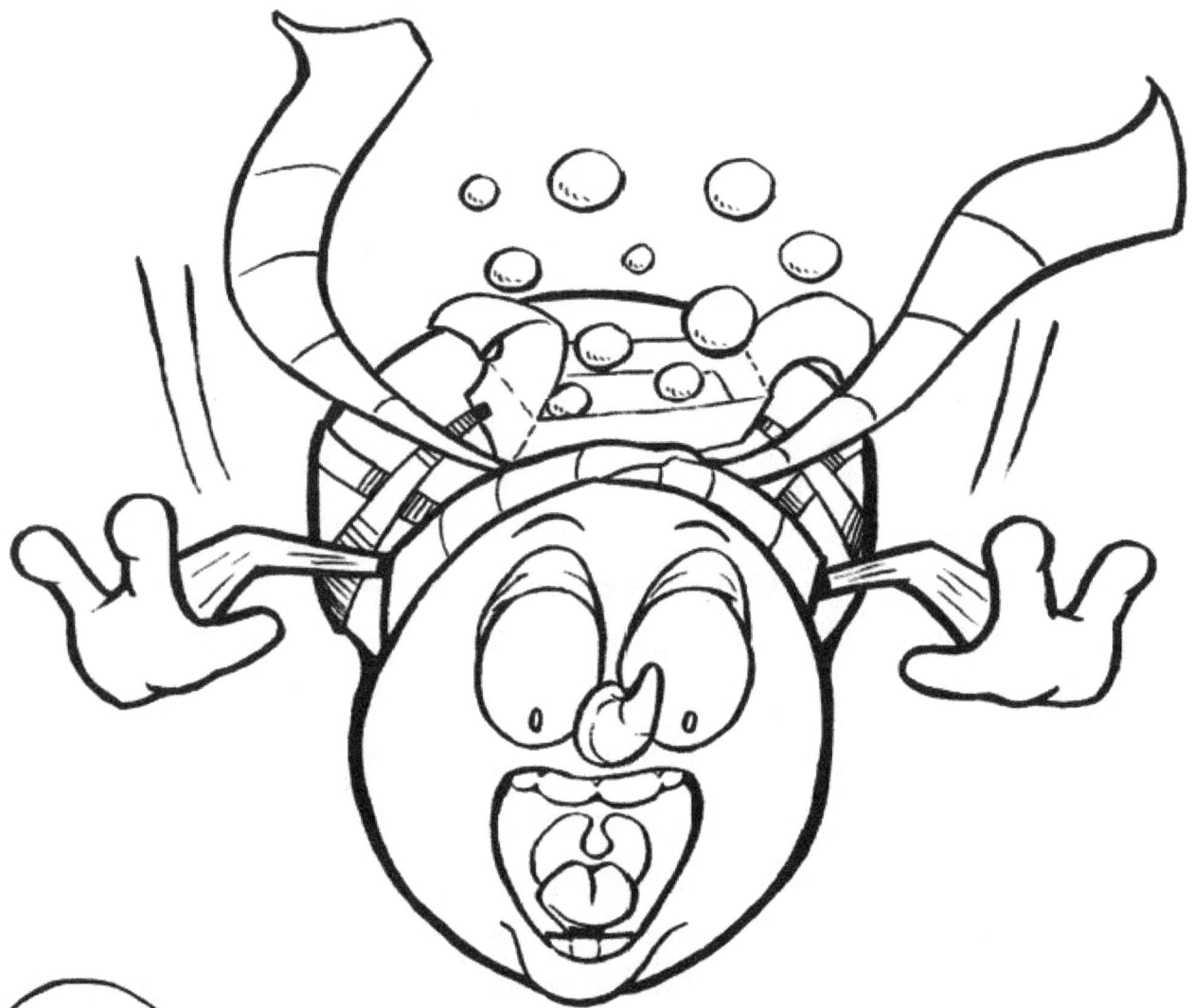

A SNOW-WOMAN WAS THE RALLYING CRY FOR TROOPS DURING THE FRENCH REVOLUTION (1870)   DON'T LOSE YOUR HEAD

FUN FACTS: YOU BURN ABOUT 238 CALORIES - JUST BUILDING THE AVERAGE SNOWMAN! GO AHEAD, START A NEW EXERCISE CRAZE

PG 23

SNOW'S GARAGE

FUN FACTS!

A NEW YORK MAN OWNS THE PATENT ON A "SNOWMAN BUILDING TOOL" (2011) ORDER YOURS TODAY! OPERATORS ARE STANDING BY!

FUN FACTS:

THERE ARE ENGINEERING BLUEPRINTS ON "HOW TO BUILD THE PERFECT SNOWMAN"
VOLUME IS EQUAL TO HOW MUCH PIE?

END ZONE

35

FUN FACTS!

IN JAPAN, AS A GOOD LUCK CHARM, SNOWMEN ARE BUILT WITH IN A HOLE THE BELLY – WHICH HOLDS A LIT CANDLE I'M MELTING! MELTING!

PG 26

WHICH PUMPKIN WOULD YOU NAME:

•OWL EYES? •UNIBROW! •SNEAKY? •CYCLOPS?

•VAMP? •TURNIP HEAD? •GIGGLES?

"SNOWY, THE TRAVELING SNOWMAN" WAS THE FIRST BOOK ABOUT A MAGICAL SNOWMAN (1944 RUTH HERMAN) HE GOT FREQUENT "RADIO FLYER" MILES

PG 28

FUN FACTS:

BUILDING SNOWMEN IS BELIEVED TO BE ONE OF THE FEW TRADITIONS WE SHARE WITH OUR DISTANT ANCESTORS! THAT AND BOOGERS

PG 29

FUN FACTS!

THE GERMAN SNOWMAN - DER SCHNEEMAN - IS CHASED BY A DOG, UNTIL HE MELTS

FLUFFY ALWAYS GETS HER MAN!

PG 30

FUN FACTS:

THE RECORD FOR MOST SNOWMEN BUILT
IN ONE PLACE (SAPPORO JAPAN) IS 12,379!

IT'S GETTING CROWDED IN HERE!

FUN FACTS:

THE WORLDS LARGEST SNOWBALL FIGHT WAS HELD IN SASKATOON (CANADA) AND HAD 7,681 PARTICIPANTS! (2016) HOPE THEY GOT HOT CHOCOLATE

PG 32

SNOWFLAKE MATCH

FUN FACTS!

FAIRY TALE & CHILDREN'S BOOK AUTHOR, HANS CHRISTIAN ANDERSEN HELPED MAKE SNOWMEN A HOLIDAY FAVORITE IN ENGLAND
TAKE THAT - FATHER CHRISTMAS!

PG 34

FUN FACTS!

NEW YEARS DAY, 1857, ARTIST LARKIN MEAD MADE A SNOWMAN SO LIFE-LIKE THAT SCHOOL BOYS REFUSED TO THROW SNOWBALLS AT IT!

NOW - GET OFF MY LAWN!

PG 35

WHAT DO YOU GET
WHEN YOU CROSS
A SNOWMAN
WITH A SHARK?

FROSTBITE!

WHAT DOES A
SNOWMAN CALL
HIS PARENTS?

MOM AND
POP-SICLE!

WHY WAS THE
SNOWMAN'S DOG
CALLED FROST?

BECAUSE
FROST BITES!

SNOWFLAKE MATCH

FIND YOUR WAY
TO THE SNOWMAN!

HERE I AM!

www.ingramcontent.com/pod-product-compliance
Lightning Source LLC
Chambersburg PA
CBHW051348290326

41933CB00042B/3336

www.ingramcontent.com/pod-product-compliance
Lightning Source LLC
Chambersburg PA
CBHW051345290326
41933CB00042B/3241